LEARNING SKILLS

Games and activities to help make
learning more effective

Denis Ballance

A Piccolo Original
Piccolo Books

A note to parents

This book is designed for children between the ages of 7-10+ years. It could have been called 'Learning to Learn', as it deals with the skills children need to make their learning a cross range of skills easier and more effective.

Learning skills are largely concerned with collecting information and assembling it in forms which assist understanding and memorizing. Many of the skills deal with comprehension of one kind or another: understanding the written word, putting data into logical order, picking out the main points of a passage, 'skimming' or reading text for a particular purpose and inferring information which is not specifically stated.

The effective use of resource material of all kinds (reference books, maps, historic documents, etc.) is another vital learning skill. In the book there is guidance on choosing likely sources of information and practical hints on making use of an index and lists of contents. Understanding pictorial and diagramatical sources of information, such as maps, charts and block graphs is also fully covered. Practice is provided in converting written information into pictorial representation in the form of graphs, charts and flow diagrams.

The activities in the book encourage children to work at their own pace. Occasionally they may ask for help – don't give the answer right away but use questions to encourage the child to find the solution alone and give plenty of praise.

The pages can be done in any order. Some may be slightly more difficult than others, so don't let the child get bogged down. The activities are there to be enjoyed. When they stop being fun, it is time for a rest and a change. So encourage the child to work in short bursts and don't let the exercises become a chore.

The parent notes on some of the pages give useful advice about the activities if you wish to work more closely with the child. (In order to avoid using 'he/she, him/her'in this book, we have referred to the child as 'she' in these notes).

The work is presented in a form which children should find interesting and enjoyable. It will be all the more enjoyable and valuable if you are willing to become actively involved in what your child is doing. The puzzles and activities should provide considerable motivation in themselves, but this motivation will be greatly enhanced by your encouragement, interest and – above all – praise.

All the answers can be found on pages 31 and 32.

1 Snoop and Pry are spies. Their job is to find things out and solve problems. Their chief is called Spymaster. Can you help them to solve their very first secret code problem?

Spymaster has told them to practise making code words by writing the missing letters from these alphabets in the spaces at the end of each line.

(1) a b c d e f g h i j k l m n o p q r s t u v w x y z   _____
(2) a b c d e f g h i j k l m n o p q r s t u v w x y z   _____
(3) a b c d e f g h i j k l m n o p q r s t u v w x y z   _____

2 Help Snoop and Pry to solve this crossword puzzle. Spymaster says that when the letters of the clues are put into **alphabetical order**, they will make real words to fit the spaces.

Across
(1) milf (3) logw
(6) stirf (10) rylog
(11) stom

Down
(1) trof (2) wol
(3) hotsg (4) tpo
(5) rytdi (7) nith
(8) oag (9) oeg

Check that the child knows the alphabet thoroughly by asking questions such as, 'Which letter comes before t?', 'Which letter follows j?'.

1 Make words by writing these sets of letters in **alphabetical order**.

| c s t o | | e s b t | | n c h i | |

2 To put words which begin with the same letter in alphabetical order, we have to look at the second or even the third letters. Look at the third letter in each word in this alphabetical list.

baby   bacon   bad   baffle   bag   bait   ball   bamboo   banana

Write these names in alphabetical order.

Heald   Hall   Hughes   Holt   _____

Anson   Agate   Adler   Antler   _____

India   Iran   Iceland   Iraq   _____

rabbit   rhino   rat   racoon   _____

3 Spymaster says, "When you have to find a name in a list which is written in alphabetical order, you can save time by starting to look in roughly the right place."
In which part of a list would you look for these words? Write beginning, middle or end after each word.

Brazil   _____   clock   _____   watch   _____

nurse   _____   zebra   _____   lily   _____

Davies   _____   violin   _____   ear   _____

magnet   _____   yarn   _____   oxygen   _____

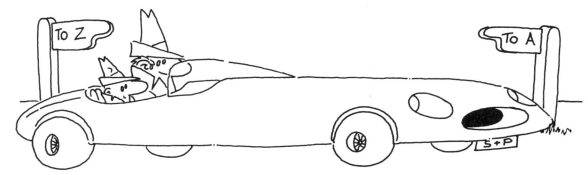

acid citric 28	diesel oil 36
acid nitric 28	dyes 39
air 45	emerald 14
alcohol 21	evaporation 45
alkali 30	fertilisers 47
atom 5	filter paper 2
baking powder 32	glass 25
carbon 12	gold 18
carbon dioxide 15	graphite 12
caustic soda 31	hard water 34
chalk 33	iodine 50
chemical change 8	lead 18
citric acid 28	lime 33
coal 36	lime water 34
coke 36	mercury 18
colour 42	minerals 17
crystals 8	metals 18
diamonds 14	

1 This is part of the **index** for a science book. It is arranged in alphabetical order and a page number is written next to each entry. Which page could you turn to find the facts about:

acids? ____ chalk? ____

glass? ____ iodine? ____

precious stones? ____

colours and dyes? ____

2 Which two pages could you try to find out whether:

(a) lime is an alkali?

_____

(b) coal is a mineral?

_____

3 Spymaster has ordered Snoop and Pry to solve some problems. Which two pages should they look up to find out whether:

(a) diamonds can be used to cut panes of

glass? _____ and _____

(b) alcohol and mercury are used in

thermometers? _____ and _____

(c) lead pencils are made of lead or

graphite? _____ and _____

The key words in this report are printed in heavy type and each line has been given a number. Read the report through and then follow the instructions given below to make an index of the key words.

(1) **Spymaster's** deadly enemy is Dr **Axel**, the head of **Berengaria's**
(2) secret service. Dr **Axel** has many secrets to hide. The most
(3) important one is **Berengaria's** new **helicopter**-launched **clockwork**
(4) **rocket**. It was invented by Professor **Isenback**. The **rocket** is
(5) code-named **SCUM**. For months, no one could find out what the
(6) name stood for, but **Snoop** and **Pry** broke the code and discovered
(7) that it meant Secret **Clockwork** Unmanned **Missile**.
(8) Queen **Donnabella** of **Berengaria** was livid when she heard that the
(9) code had been broken. She ordered **Axel** to report to the **Grimslot**
(10) Palace in her capital city of **Elsborg** and fined him 2,000 **flottis**.

Write the key words on scrap paper. Arrange them in alphabetical order. Make the words into an index for the report by writing them below in the correct order. Put the number of the line where each word appears next to it in the index. Many of the words need more than one number.

A _____   F _____   P _____

_____   _____   _____

_____   _____   S _____

_____   _____   S _____

E _____   M _____   S _____

1 Five of the words in each of these sets begin and end with the same letter. Underline the five words in each set.

(1) those that thatch treat them twist throat thing tight this
(2) high heath harpoon heather holly harvest harsh health hutch
(3) lift lock large level label local lever listen legal loyal

2 Look at the twenty words in the box. Think about their meanings. Sort the words into four sets. There are five words in each. Write each set of five words into one of the boxes below. When you have filled each box, write a title for the set at the top.

peach silver pear coat
deer iron skirt orange
panda gold shirt apple
steel mouse socks goat
shorts brass wolf plum

Sorting and classifying are valuable skills. These exercises give practice in classifying by word shape and meaning.

1 Pry saw a girl handing a letter to an agent of Dr Axel. The girl was tall, fair-haired and wearing spectacles. When he got back to base, Spymaster showed Pry this checklist of four suspects who were known to be working for Dr Axel. What is the code name of the girl Pry saw?

code name

code name	male	female	tall	short	fair hair	dark hair	wears spectacles
Rondo		✓	✓		✓		
Novak		✓				✓	✓
Leroy	✓		✓		✓		✓
Hildi		✓	✓		✓		✓

2 Four of Dr Axel's agents were asked to name three features they wanted in a small car.
These were their answers.

A I want four doors, electric windows and a trouble-free diesel engine.
B My choice is a roomy hatchback with two doors and a petrol engine.
C A diesel-powered car with four doors and a hatchback is what I want.
D I need a very large boot and central locking for all four doors.

Tick three boxes on each line of this chart to show the drivers' choices.

driver	four doors	two doors	diesel engine	petrol engine	hatch-back	large boot	electric windows	central locking
A								
B								
C								
D								

Discussion points: When might you use a checklist like this? What about catalogues, holiday brochures, etc?

1 Sally Boxwatch likes animals. Which of these programmes would she enjoy? _____

```
5-00   PUPPET THEATRE   The Noodles – fun for the under-fives
5-30   ZOO PARADE   Monthly zoo magazine for children of all ages
6-00   NATIONAL NEWS
6-20   REGIONAL REVIEW – news from the Regions
6-30   BARNEY BOODLES BRAINSTORM   Family quiz show
7-00   LAKESIDE, ILLINOIS   Long-running soap opera from the U.S.A.
7-45   MUSTANG   Australian documentary on threatened wild horses
8-30   LANDSCAPE   Fast Food! Slow Death? Enquiry into snack foods
9-15   YOUR TURN – Viewers' views of last week's TV programmes
9-45   FILM   The Battle for Burma – action packed story of the campaign
```

2 During the evening, each member of Sally's family watched two programmes. Which ones do you think they chose? Write the two programme names here.

Mrs Boxwatch likes American soap operas and quiz games.

_____
_____

Mr Boxwatch enjoys old war films and the local news.

_____
_____

Dawn Boxwatch supports the World Wild Life Fund. She will only eat health foods.

_____
_____

This exercise tests comprehension and classifying skills.
When your child has completed this activity, ask her to look at the TV programmes for the week and to draw up a list of family favourites.

1

In this puzzle, each row across contains five words and also the name of the **group** they belong to. Colour the group name box in each row.

banana	peach	apricot	fruit	apple	orange
pansy	lupin	flower	poppy	tulip	violet
lime	tree	walnut	beech	birch	poplar
colour	pink	carmine	green	blue	yellow
copper	iron	silver	steel	zinc	metal
baboon	wolf	camel	horse	animal	sheep
coal	oil	charcoal	fuel	wood	coke

2 Test your memory

Study this picture carefully. Then turn to the page opposite and answer the questions. Allow yourself one minute to study the picture.

Please check the time carefully. For a younger child allow two minutes.

1 Test your memory

(1) What is the name of the street? _____

(2) How many people could you see? _____

(3) What number is the tallest house? _____

(4) Which house has a fire burning? _____

(5) What is painted on No. 13's garage? _____

(6) Which dog is nearer to the lamp post, the big one or the little one? _____

(7) How many birds are sitting on the wires? _____

(8) What is the man on the ladder mending? _____

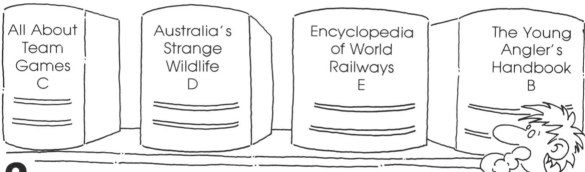

2
The reference books shown on this page have been given letters. Use the letters as answers. Which book would you use to find out about these?

(1) Grey kangaroos _____

(2) Netball rules _____

(3) Steam trains _____

(4) Coarse fishing _____

(5) Irish railways _____

(6) The best way to catch trout and salmon _____

(7) The history of Rugby Union Football _____

> Discussion points: Where are reference books kept in your local library? Ask your child to think of some of the different topic sections.

1 Look at this picture of Merton Street and fill in the missing numbers in the description below.

(1) Mrs Adey has flowers all around her house.

She lives at Number _____ .

(2) Mr Ford's tall house has two storeys and an attic.

It is Number _____ .

(3) Mr Bell's house, Number _____ , used to be the village shop.

(4) Miss Carr lives in a flat above a lock-up garage.

Her number is _____ .

(5) Old Mrs Gee feels the cold and always has a fire.

Her number is _____ .

(6) Mrs Dean lives at Number Nine, next door to

Miss Eton at Number _____ .

2 The plan at the bottom is a bird's eye view of Merton Street. Write the number of each house in the circle and the owner's name in the square.

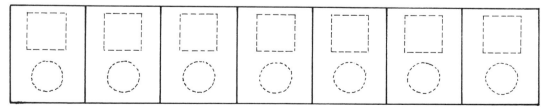

Merton Street

12

These are the people who live at one end of Merton Street. Their ages are given in brackets. We can make lists of the people who live in the street in many different ways. Write the names in the correct places in each list.

No. 1	Mrs Adey (66)
No. 3	Mrs Gee (79), Mr C King (33), Mrs Y King (30)
No. 5	Mr R Bell (41), Mrs T Bell (38), Anne Bell (14), James Bell (9)
No. 7	Mr L Ford (49), Mrs B Ford (45), Mark Ford (19), Jane Ford (15)

People who live in Merton Street

males and females	by ages	in alphabetical order
Males	Over 60	(Mr R Bell comes before Mrs T Bell because R comes before T)
	18 to 60	
Females		
	Under 18	

Pretend that you are Snoop's partner, Pry, and that you are hiding behind a tree and overhear what happens in this story. You will have to make a report to Spymaster on how Snoop came to be caught. Now read the story.

Snoop was staying near the SCUM secret weapon factory in Western Berengaria. He was disguised as a butterfly collector. One night, two agents of Dr Axel caught him snooping around near the factory.

"Who are you?" one of them demanded. "And what are you doing?"

"I am Professor Hawkweed, the world's leading expert on butterflies," said Snoop. "I'm out looking for butterflies."

"I don't believe you," the second agent said. "Any fool knows that you don't find butterflies flying at night."

"Are you trying to teach me my job?" Snoop said angrily. "Look at these butterflies. I've caught them tonight."

"They're moths!" the agent sneered. "Hands up! You're under arrest."

These are Spymaster's questions. Write answers to them.

(1) Where was Snoop caught? _____

(2) What name was he using? _____

(3) How was he disguised? _____

(4) What time of day was it? _____

(5) How did Snoop try to prove his story? _____
_____

(6) How did the agent know that Snoop was lying? _____
_____

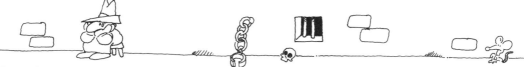

1 Read these sentences.

Snoop was in Dr Axel's prison. One day the jailer brought him a parcel. Inside was a box of long thin chocolates, called Thinmints, and a very strange letter.

The letter said, 'Friend in Lagos expects to open café. Unless trade bad abroad, results seen in next month. I need ten pounds. Reply yesterday.' Snoop puzzled over the words for ages and decided that it was a coded message.

He tried to remember how Pry's code worked. Snoop had failed the spy's code examination. Finally he gave up and ate one of the mints.

It was very good. By tea-time, there were only three left – out of fifty! He decided to have one more before tea and save the rest.

Snoop bit into the mint. There was a very loud crack. He had broken a tooth. Inside the mint there was something very hard. It was made of steel and it had nasty rough edges.

Answer these questions.

(1) What was in the parcel?

_____

(2) What did Snoop think the letter must be?

_____

(3) Who did Snoop think the letter might be from?

_____

(4) How many Thinmints had Snoop eaten by tea-time?

_____

(5) Can you guess what was inside the Thinmint?

_____

2 Then Snoop remembered the code! To break it, write the first letter of each word in the message on these lines.

_____

_____

_____

Listing in alphabetical order is a very good way to arrange sets of names, words and topics. Match these sets of names and words with the books and lists they are taken from.

1
Barker J.B, 17 Queen St.	...605348
Barker J.T, 18 Manor Rd.	...606233
Barman Rev. P, 8 Corbett St.	...606007
Barnaby K, Roedean House	...603115

2
Melbourne, Australia	19, 49
Melbourne, Lord	543, 544
Mercury (planet)	68, 69, 70
meteorites	467 (plate 44)

3
Adams, Mary Christine	16 – 9 – 81
Bassi, Hardib Kaur	7 – 7 – 82
Brown, Andrew Marcus	12 – 1 – 82
Bunbury, Simon Rupert	4 – 4 – 82

4
Dogs, Cape Hunting	46
Elephant, African	26, 27
Gazelle, Grant's	86
Gnu (or wildebeeste)	77

5
finish (v) To bring to an end
fir (n) Evergreen coniferous tree
fire 1. (n) Mass of burning material
     2. (v) To shoot with a gun

(a) Class List Form 2B Ravensmoor School

(b) Animals of the African Plains — Index

(c) TELEPHONE DIRECTORY East Charnley

(d) Encyclopedia of Everyday Knowledge — Index

(e) Easier English Dictionary T. Coote

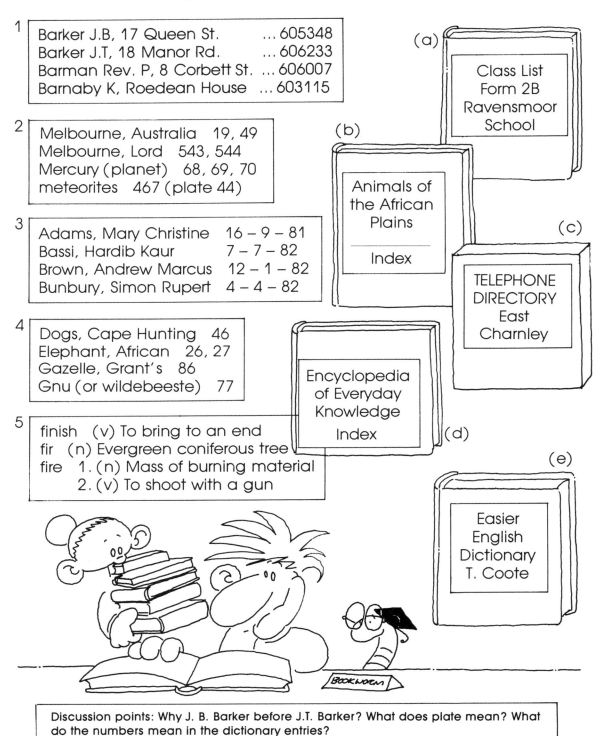

Discussion points: Why J. B. Barker before J.T. Barker? What does plate mean? What do the numbers mean in the dictionary entries?

1 Most dictionaries have **head words** on their pages. They look like this:

SAIL   SANDAL

The head words are the first and last words on each page. They help us to find words quickly. If you are looking for salamander, you know that the words beginning with sal- will be on the page which has SAIL and SANDAL as head words.

Draw a line from each of these words to the head words of the dictionary page where you would find it.

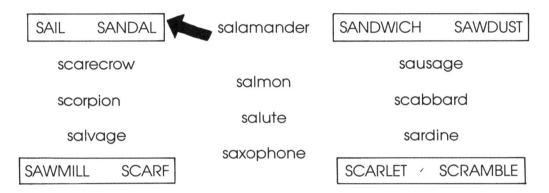

2 Look up these words in a dictionary. Write their meanings on the lines and the head words of the pages where you find them in the boxes.

optician _____

rubble _____

dormitory _____

jubilant _____

17

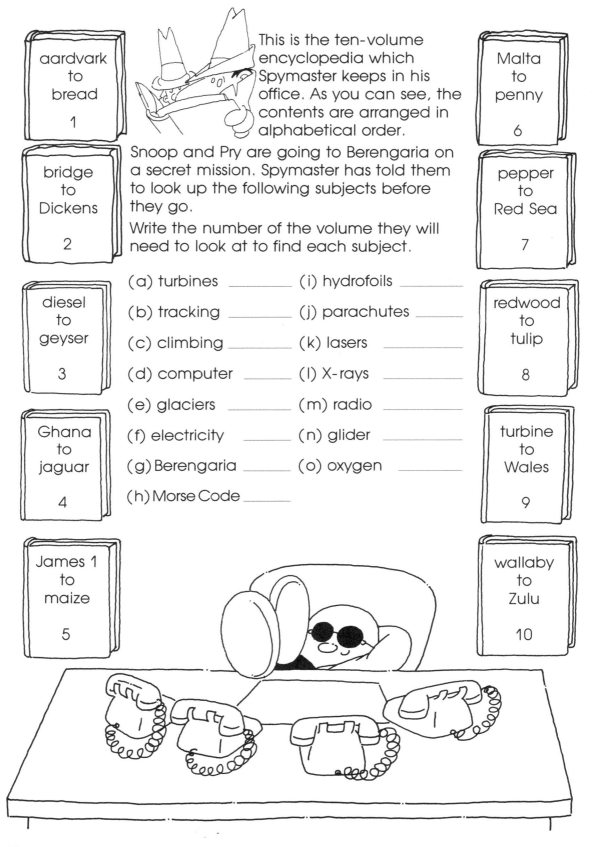

aardvark to bread — 1

bridge to Dickens — 2

diesel to geyser — 3

Ghana to jaguar — 4

James 1 to maize — 5

Malta to penny — 6

pepper to Red Sea — 7

redwood to tulip — 8

turbine to Wales — 9

wallaby to Zulu — 10

This is the ten-volume encyclopedia which Spymaster keeps in his office. As you can see, the contents are arranged in alphabetical order.

Snoop and Pry are going to Berengaria on a secret mission. Spymaster has told them to look up the following subjects before they go.

Write the number of the volume they will need to look at to find each subject.

(a) turbines _____
(b) tracking _____
(c) climbing _____
(d) computer _____
(e) glaciers _____
(f) electricity _____
(g) Berengaria _____
(h) Morse Code _____
(i) hydrofoils _____
(j) parachutes _____
(k) lasers _____
(l) X-rays _____
(m) radio _____
(n) glider _____
(o) oxygen _____

1 Read these sentences carefully. Look out for facts about seeds.

Pines, firs, spruces and larches are called coniferous trees.

Larches lose their leaves in winter but the other coniferous trees stay green all the year round. The long, thin leaves are called needles.

All coniferous trees grow cones on their branches, Their seeds are found between the scales of the cones. While the seeds are growing, the scales are green and tightly closed. When the seeds are ripe, the scales turn brown and stand out from the sides of the cone.

The open cones are shaken by the wind and thousands of tiny seeds fall out. So tiny are the seeds that they can travel for hundreds of metres on the wind before falling to the ground.

2 In each sentence, cross out the words from the brackets which are wrong.

(1) The seeds of coniferous trees are (very small/very large).
(2) The seeds are found (on the needles/between the cone scales).
(3) While the seeds are growing, the cone scales are (brown/green).
(4) When the seeds are ripe, the scales (fall off/open out).
(5) The seeds of coniferous trees are spread by (insects/the wind).
(6) All coniferous trees (stay green all the year round/produce cones).

Choose words from the box to complete the labels on these pictures.

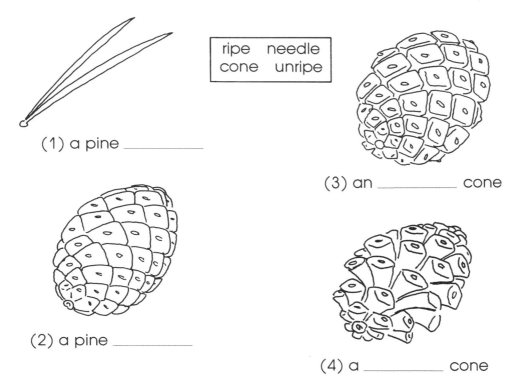

ripe   needle
cone   unripe

(1) a pine _____

(2) a pine _____

(3) an _____ cone

(4) a _____ cone

1 Underline the one word in each of these groups which does not fit in with the others.

(1) apple   egg   pear   grapefruit   peach
(2) pork   cheese   beef   lamb   mutton
(3) tiger   leopard   jaguar   lion   wolf
(4) wool   linen   silk   nylon   cotton
(5) copper   glass   steel   aluminium   tin
(6) emerald   diamond   pearl   opal   ruby

2 Spymaster says, "A good spy should always be able to spot anything which does not fit in with the things around it."

Can you spot something in each of these pictures which does not fit in? Draw it in the small box.

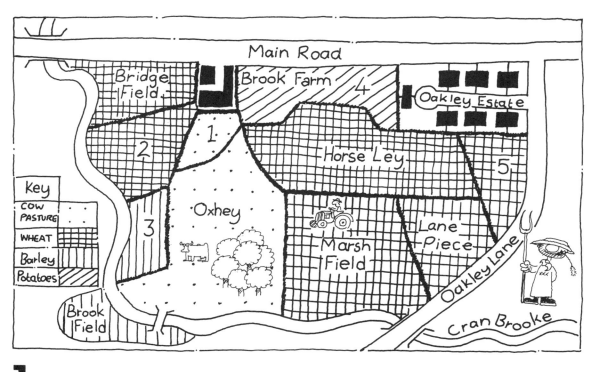

1 This is Brook Farm. Some of the fields have names. Others have numbers.

(1) How many fields are alongside a road? _____

(2) How many fields are next to a stream? _____

(3) How many fields are grazed by cattle? _____

(4) Which two fields grow a grain crop which is not wheat? _____ _____

(5) Oakley Estate houses are semi-detached. How many are there?

(6) Which field is this? _____

2 Complete each of these sentences.

(1) The field between the farmhouse and Oakley Estate grows _____ .

(2) There is a small wood in the middle of the field called _____ .

(3) The farmer must cross a bridge over the stream to reach _____ .

(4) The farmer uses more than half of his land for growing _____ .

Spymaster told Snoop to travel to Istanbul on the Balkan Express. This is his timetable for the trip.

London	0030
Dover	0150
Calais	0400
Paris	0600
Lyons	1000
Milan	1730
Venice	2030
Zagreb	0230
Belgrade	0500
Sofia	1000
Istanbul	1700

Here are some of the things which happened on the journey. Write the numbers 1 to 10 in the spaces to show the <u>order</u> in which they took place.

(a) Snoop boarded the train at London Victoria Station. _____

(b) Snoop caught up some sleep between Paris and Lyons. _____

(c) Pry met his friend Snoop on the platform at Sofia. _____

(d) An agent of Dr Axel boarded the train in Paris. _____

(e) Snoop lost his briefcase between Venice and Zagreb. _____

(f) Snoop sent a telegram to Pry when he reached Milan. _____

(g) A blizzard delayed the train between Lyons and Milan. _____

(h) Dr Axel's secret agent left the train at Belgrade. _____

(i) Snoop reached Istanbul late on Wednesday afternoon. _____

(j) The travellers crossed the sea from Dover to Calais. _____

This exercise gives practice in sequencing or putting the parts of a narrative in the correct order.

Flow diagrams are used to give instructions and to place facts in order. This flow diagram is a step-by-step explanation of how to make concrete.

| Take three buckets of sand. | → | Add one bucket of gravel. | → | Add one bucket of cement. |

| Mix with a clean spade. | → | Add water a little at a time | → | Mix until the concrete will spread. |

1 These instructions are for making a cup of tea. They are in the wrong order. Write them into the flow diagram in the correct order.

(1) Put three tea bags in the teapot.
(2) Stir tea in cup with a spoon.
(3) Leave to brew for five minutes.
(4) Put sufficient milk in the cup.
(5) Warm the teapot with hot water.
(6) Pour boiling water over tea bags.
(7) Fill a kettle with fresh water.
(8) Pour tea from teapot into cup.
(9) Boil the water in the kettle.

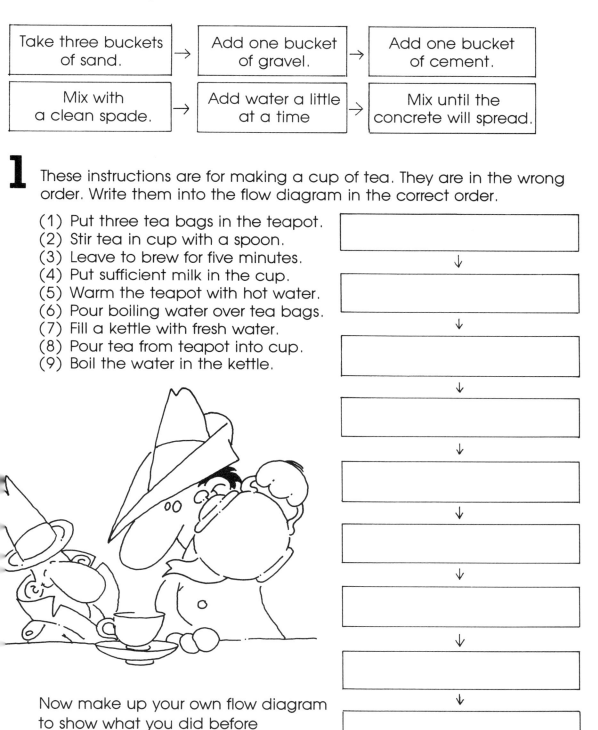

Now make up your own flow diagram to show what you did before you had your breakfast this morning.

23

1 This diagram shows two of the highest mountains in each of the six continents. Choose a colour for each continent and, with the help of the chart, shade each mountain to show which continent it is in.

| Australasia | N. America | Asia |
| Mauna Loa | Mt. McKinley | Mt. Everest |
Carstensz	Popocatepetl	Godwin-Austen
Africa	S. America	Europe
Mt. Kenya	Aconcagua	Mont Blanc
Kilimanjaro	Chimborazo	Monte Rosa

2 Complete this diagram which shows some of the world's longest rivers. Allow one centimetre on the paper for each 250 miles of river.

River Nile   4,000 miles

Mississippi   3,750 miles

Yangtse Kiang   3,250 miles

Congo   3,000 miles

Yellow River   2,500 miles

> The river lengths are approximate. You may need to help with scales.

1 The map below is covered with squares. These squares are called a **grid**. We use the grid to fix the positions of places on the map.
To read a grid reference number, we first count the lines across and then follow a line up the map until we reach the correct place.
The windmill on this map is at Reference 6F. What can you see at:

(a) Reference 3D? _____ (b) Reference 8B? _____

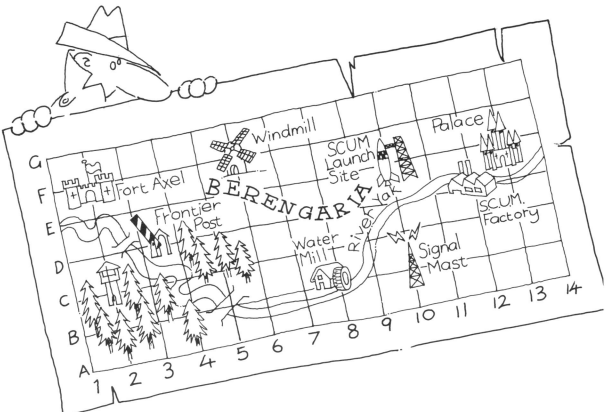

2 Spymaster told Pry to meet Snoop in the building at 2C. Put an X by it. To reach the frontier of Berengaria, they had to walk through the forest to the river bridge at 5B. Then they had to follow these map references: 6C 7C 8D 9E 10E. Mark their route with a felt tip or crayon line.

(1) What did Snoop and Pry find at Reference 10E? _____

(2) What is the grid reference of the SCUM factory? _____

(3) They had to avoid the Queen's palace. What is its reference? _____

(4) Snoop and Pry blew up the structure at 10B. What was it? _____

25

1 These figures show the number of young trees planted in Britain during a recent year.

Spruce – 41 000 000   Fir and Larch – 15 000 000   Pine – 23 000 000
Oak and Beech – 1 000 000   Total number of trees 80 000 000

Show this information on a **picture diagram**. There are eighty squares on the grid below. Let each square stand for 1 000 000 trees. Colour in the correct number of squares for each kind of tree. Colour the key squares in the same colours. Use four different colours. To make the picture diagram clearer, draw tree symbols in a few squares in each section.

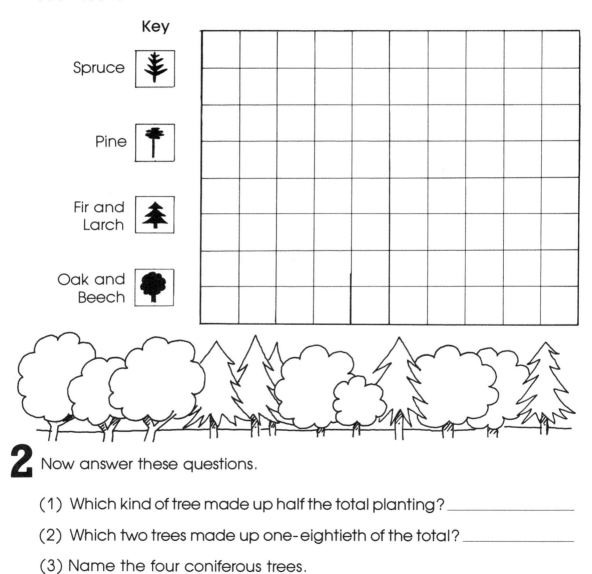

2 Now answer these questions.

(1) Which kind of tree made up half the total planting? _____

(2) Which two trees made up one-eightieth of the total? _____

(3) Name the four coniferous trees.
_____

1 This picture diagram is a **block graph.** It shows how the people who live in Merton Street travel to work. Each square stands for one person.

(1) Which is the most popular way to get to work? _____

(2) How many people are able to walk or cycle to work? _____

Means	Number of people
bus	
car	
cycle	
m/cycle	
on foot	

2 If the figures to be shown on a block graph are very large, one square may be used to stand for a number of items. This graph shows the attendance at a large school for one week. <u>One square stands for 20 people.</u> The attendance for Monday was: 27 squares x 20 = 540 children.

Each ☐ stands for 20 people.

Mon	Tues	Wed	Thurs	Fri

(1) How many children were at school on Tuesday? _____

(2) How many children were at school on Friday? _____

(3) Which was the best day for attendance? _____

(4) On which day was the attendance lowest? _____

Block graphs may be vertical or horizontal. Colour in the blocks.

The block graph on this page shows the population of each country in the European Economic Community (Common Market). Study the chart below and fill in the names of the countries in the correct places. Colour the blocks.

Population in millions

Belgium	10	Denmark	5	Greece	6	Netherlands	13
Britain	55	France	51	Italy	54	Portugal	10
Eire	3	Germany	62	Luxembourg	0.3	Spain	34

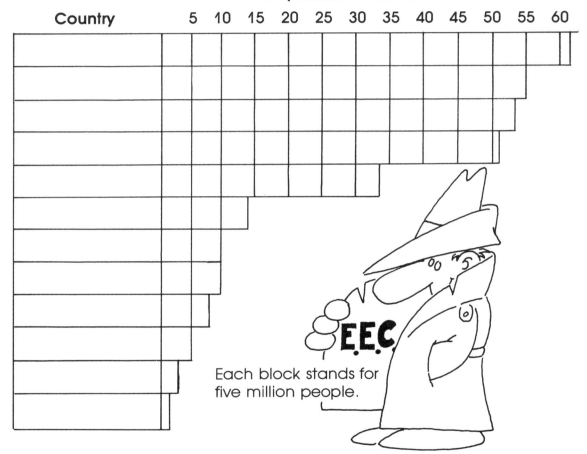

Each block stands for five million people.

motorcycle

Sometimes, symbols take the place of blocks. Design simple symbols for these:

| people | aeroplane | car |

1

Tom Davis is now fifteen. This chart shows his height at various ages. Use the data to complete this **graph**. →

Height					
cm	80	100	120	140	160
Age	7	9	11	13	15

Colour in the correct number of blocks in each column.

Height in centimetres →

(Graph axes: vertical marked 20, 40, 60, 80, 100, 120, 140, 160; horizontal Age: 7, 9, 11, 13, 15)

2 Test your memory

In spite of his broken tooth, Snoop filed away one of the bars in his cell and escaped from the prison where Dr Axel was holding him.

Next day, he got into the SCUM factory dressed in his tea lady disguise. While he was snooping around the Chief Engineer's office, he saw this drawing. Snoop had two minutes to remember it.

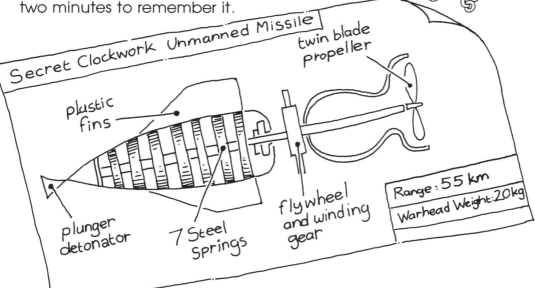

Give yourself two minutes to study the plan. Then turn to the next page.

1 Test your memory

(1) What were the fins made of? _____

(2) What were the springs made of? _____

How many:

(3) blades had the propeller? _____

(4) kilograms did the warhead weigh? _____

(5) springs were inside? _____

(6) kilometres could the missile fly? _____

(7) Which two jobs did this part do? ⊐╟⊏ _____ _____

(8) What kind of detonator was fitted to the nose? _____

2 Find the odd one out in each of these sets of four words. Write your answers into the correct spaces in the crossword puzzle below.

Across
(1) water sawdust milk vinegar
(2) copper steel glass silver
(5) crimson scarlet indigo red
(6) lemon tangerine orange peach
(7) piccolo violin cello guitar

Down
(1) taxicab car tractor sledge
(3) Spain France Mexico Germany

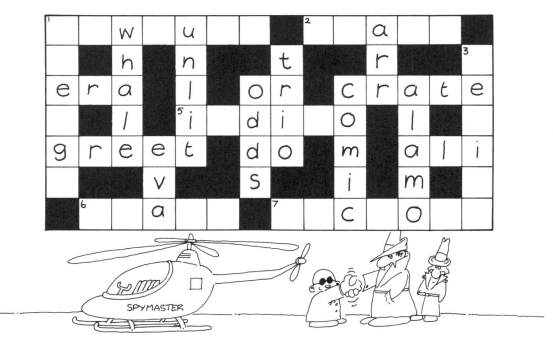

30

Answers

Page 3
1 (1) lost (2) city (3) know
2 **Across** (1) film (3) glow (6) first
(10) glory (11) most
Down (1) fort (2) low (3) ghost (4) opt
(5) dirty (7) hint (8) ago (9) ego

Page 4
1 cost, best, chin, chimp
2 Hall, Heald, Holt, Hughes
Adler, Agate, Anson, Antler
Iceland, India, Iran, Iraq
rabbit, racoon, rat, rhino
3

beginning	middle	end
Brazil	nurse	zebra
Davies	magnet	violin
clock	lily	yarn
ear	oxygen	watch

Page 5
1 acids 28, chalk 33, glass 25, iodine 50,
precious stones 8/14,
colours and dyes 42/39
2 (a) 30/33, (b) 17/36
3 (a) 14/25, (b) 18/21, (c) 12/18

Page 6
A Axel (1/2/9)
B Berengaria (1/3/8)
C clockwork (3/7)
D Donnabella (8)
E Elsborg (10)
F flottis (10)
G Grimslot (9)
H helicopter (3)
I Isenback
M Missile (7)
P Pry (6)
R rocket (4)
S Scum (5)
Snoop (6)
Spymaster (1)

Page 7
1 (1) that, treat, twist, throat, tight
(2) high, heath, harsh, health, hutch
(3) level, label, local, legal, loyal
2 **Fruit** peach, pear, orange, apple, plum
Metal silver, iron, gold, steel, brass
Clothes coat, skirt, shirt, socks, shorts
Animals deer, panda, mouse, goat, wolf

Page 8
1 Code name: Hildi

Page 9
1 Zoo Parade, Mustang
2 **Mrs Boxwatch:** Barney Boodles Brainstorm,
Lakeside, Illinois
Mr Boxwatch: The Battle for Burma,
Regional Review
Dawn: Mustang, Landscape

Page 10
1 fruit, flower, tree, colour, metal,
animal, fuel

Page 11
1 (1) Merton Street (2) Three people
(3) No. 7 (4) No. 9 (5) Keep Clear
(6) The big one. (7) Three. (8) An aerial.
2 (1) D (2) C (3) E (4) B (5) E (6) B (7) C

Page 12
1 (1) 1 (2) 7 (3) 5 (4) 13 (5) 3 (6) 11

Page 13
Males: Mr C King, Mr R Bell, James Bell,
Mr L Ford, Mark Ford
Females: Mrs Adey, Mrs Gee, Mrs Y King,
Mrs T Bell, Anne Bell, Mrs B Ford, Jane Ford
Over 60: Mrs Gee, Mrs Adey
18-60: Mr C King, Mrs Y King, Mr R Bell,
Mrs T Bell, Mr L Ford, Mrs B Ford, Mark Ford
Under 18: Anne Bell, James Bell, Jane Ford
Alphabetical order: Mrs Adey, Anne Bell,
James Bell, Mr R Bell, Mrs T Bell, Mrs B Ford,
Jane Ford, Mr L Ford, Mark Ford, Mrs Gee,
Mr C King, Mrs Y King

Page 14
(1) Near the SCUM secret weapon factory.
(2) Professor Hawkweed
(3) As a butterfly collector
(4) It was night.
(5) He showed them insects in his net.
(6) The insects were moths.

Page 15
1 (1) chocolates, a letter
(2) a coded message (3) Pry (4) 48
(5) a file
2 File to cut bars in mint Pry

Page 16
1 (c), 2 (d), 3 (a), 4 (b), 5 (e)

Page 17
1 SAIL – SANDAL salamander, salmon,
salute, salvage
SAWMILL – SCARF saxophone, scabbard,
scarecrow
SANDWICH – SAWDUST sardine, sausage
SCARLET – SCRAMBLE scorpion

Page 18
(a) 9, (b) 8, (c) 2, (d) 2, (e) 4, (f) 3, (g) 1,
(h) 6, (i) 5, (j) 6, (k) 5, (l) 10, (m) 7,
(n) 4, (o) 6

Page 19
1 (1) very small (2) between the cone scales
(3) green (4) open out (5) the wind
(6) produce cones
2 (1) needle (2) cone (3) unripe (4) ripe

Page 20
1 (1) egg (2) cheese (3) wolf (4) nylon
   (5) glass (6) pearl

Page 21
1 (1) Five (2) Six (3) Two
   (4) No. 3, Brook Field
   (5) Fourteen houses that are attached to
   each other.
   (6) Horse Ley
2 (1) potatoes (2) Oxhey (3) Brook Field
   (4) wheat

Page 22
(a) 1, (b) 4, (c) 9, (d) 3, (e) 7, (f) 6, (g) 5,
(h) 8, (i) 10, (j) 2

Page 23
1 7, 9, 5, 1, 6, 3, 4, 8, 2

Page 25
1 (a) Frontier Post (b) Water Mill
2 (1) SCUM Launch Site
   (2) 12 D
   (3) 13 E
   (4) Signal Mast

Page 26
2 (1) Spruce (2) Oak/Beach (3) Spruce,
   Pine, Fir, Larch

Page 27
1 (1) car (2) Five
2 (1) 500 (2) 440 (3) Wednesday (4) Friday

Page 30
1 (1) plastic (2) steel (3) Two (4) 20 kg
   (5) Seven (6) 55 km (7) flywheel,
   winding gear (8) plunger
3 **Across** (1) sawdust (2) glass (5) indigo
   (6) peach (7) piccolo
   Down (1) sledge (3) Mexico